5 Minute Gratitude Journal

This 5 Minute Gratitude Journal Belongs To

_____

Day _____ Date _____

Today I am **Grateful** for:

_____

_____

_____

_____

_____

_____

*"Do not spoil what you have by desiring what you
have not; remember that what you now
have was once among the things
you only hoped for."— Epicurus*

Day _____ Date _____

Today I am **Grateful** for:

_____

_____

_____

_____

_____

_____

_____

Day _____ Date _____

Today I am **Grateful** for:

_____

_____

_____

_____

_____

_____

*"Let gratitude be the pillow upon which you kneel to say
your nightly prayer. And let faith be the bridge you
build to overcome evil and welcome good."*
— Maya Angelou

Day _____ Date _____

Today I am **Grateful** for:

_____

_____

_____

_____

_____

_____

_____

Day _____ Date _____

Today I am **Grateful** for:

_____

_____

_____

_____

_____

_____

*"Acknowledging the good that you already have in
your life is the foundation for all abundance."*
— Eckhart Tolle

Day _____ Date _____

Today I am **Grateful** for:

_____

_____

_____

_____

_____

_____

_____

Day _____ Date _____

Today I am *Grateful* for:

"Forget yesterday - it has already forgotten you.
Don't sweat tomorrow - you haven't even met.
Instead, open your eyes and your heart to a truly
precious gift - today."
— Steve Maraboli

Day _____ Date _____

Today I am *Grateful* for:

Day _____ Date _____

Today I am **Grateful** for:

_____

_____

_____

_____

_____

_____

"Some people grumble that roses have thorns; I am grateful that thorns have roses."
— Alphonse Karr

Day _____ Date _____

Today I am **Grateful** for:

_____

_____

_____

_____

_____

_____

_____

Day _____ Date _____

Today I am **Grateful** for:

"Gratitude is not only the greatest of virtues, but the parent of all others."
— Marcus Tullius Cicero

Day _____ Date _____

Today I am **Grateful** for:

Day _____ Date _____

Today I am **Grateful** for:

_____

_____

_____

_____

_____

_____

"God gave you a gift of 86 400 seconds today. Have you used one to say thank you"
— *William Arthur Ward*

Day _____ Date _____

Today I am **Grateful** for:

_____

_____

_____

_____

_____

_____

Day _____ Date _____

Today I am **Grateful** for:

"Gratitude looks to the Past and love to the Present;
fear, avarice, lust, and ambition look ahead."
— C.S. Lewis

Day _____ Date _____

Today I am **Grateful** for:

Day _____ Date _____

Today I am **Grateful** for:

_____

_____

_____

_____

_____

_____

"I would maintain that thanks are the highest form of thought; and that gratitude is happiness doubled by wonder". ~G.K. Chesterton

Day _____ Date _____

Today I am **Grateful** for:

_____

_____

_____

_____

_____

_____

_____

Day _____ Date _____

Today I am *Grateful* for:

"When you are grateful, fear disappears and
abundance appears."
— Anthony Robbins

Day _____ Date _____

Today I am *Grateful* for:

Day _____ Date _____

Today I am **Grateful** for:

_____

_____

_____

_____

_____

_____

*"Feeling gratitude and not expressing it is like
wrapping a present and not giving it."*
— William Arthur Ward

Day _____ Date _____

Today I am **Grateful** for:

_____

_____

_____

_____

_____

_____

_____

Day _____ Date _____

Today I am **Grateful** for:

_____

_____

_____

_____

_____

_____

"The world is 3 days: As for yesterday, it has vanished
along with all that was in it. As for tomorrow, you
may never see it. As for today, it is yours, so work on
it." — al-Hasan al-Basri

Day _____ Date _____

Today I am **Grateful** for:

_____

_____

_____

_____

_____

_____

Day _____ Date _____

Today I am **Grateful** for:

_____

_____

_____

_____

_____

_____

"After every storm, there is a rainbow. If you have eyes, you will find it. If you have wisdom, you will create it. If you have love for yourself and others, you won't need it." — Shannon L. Alder

Day _____ Date _____

Today I am **Grateful** for:

_____

_____

_____

_____

_____

_____

_____

Day _____ Date _____

Today I am **Grateful** for:

_____

_____

_____

_____

_____

_____

"Regardless of Sunshine or Rain, Be Thankful for
another GREAT day...and treat Life as the
ULTIMATE Gift.... Because IT IS :)"
— Pablo

Day _____ Date _____

Today I am **Grateful** for:

_____

_____

_____

_____

_____

_____

_____

Day _____ Date _____

Today I am **Grateful** for:

_____

_____

_____

_____

_____

_____

"The unthankful heart discovers no mercies; but the thankful heart will find, in every hour, some heavenly blessings." — Henry Ward Beecher

Day _____ Date _____

Today I am **Grateful** for:

_____

_____

_____

_____

_____

_____

_____

Day _____ Date _____

Today I am **Grateful** for:

_____

_____

_____

_____

_____

_____

"For each new morning with its light,
For rest and shelter of the night,
For health and food, for love and friends,
For everything Thy goodness sends."
— Ralph Waldo Emerson

Day _____ Date _____

Today I am **Grateful** for:

_____

_____

_____

_____

_____

_____

Day _____ Date _____

Today I am **Grateful** for:

_____

_____

_____

_____

_____

_____

*"When it comes to life the critical thing is whether
you take things for granted or take them
with gratitude."*
— G.K. Chesterton

Day _____ Date _____

Today I am **Grateful** for:

_____

_____

_____

_____

_____

_____

_____

Day _____ Date _____

Today I am **Grateful** for:

_____

_____

_____

_____

_____

_____

*"Take full account of what Excellences you possess,
and in gratitude remember how you would hanker
after them, if you had them not."*
— Marcus Aurelius

Day _____ Date _____

Today I am **Grateful** for:

_____

_____

_____

_____

_____

_____

_____

Day _____ Date _____

Today I am **Grateful** for:

_____

_____

_____

_____

_____

_____

"I may not be where I want to be but I'm thankful for
not being where I used to be."
— Habeeb Akande

Day _____ Date _____

Today I am **Grateful** for:

_____

_____

_____

_____

_____

_____

Day _____ Date _____

Today I am *Grateful* for:

"The miracle is not to walk on water. The miracle is to walk on the green earth, dwelling deeply in the present moment and feeling truly alive."
— Thích Nhất Hạnh

Day _____ Date _____

Today I am *Grateful* for:

Day _____ Date _____

Today I am **Grateful** for:

_____

_____

_____

_____

_____

_____

"Be happy, noble heart, be blessed for all the good
thou hast done and wilt do hereafter, and let my
gratitude remain in obscurity like your good deeds."
— Alexandre Dumas

Day _____ Date _____

Today I am **Grateful** for:

_____

_____

_____

_____

_____

_____

_____

Day _____ Date _____

Today I am **Grateful** for:

"Courtesies of a small and trivial character are the
ones which strike deepest in the grateful and
appreciating heart."
— Henry Clay

Day _____ Date _____

Today I am **Grateful** for:

Day _____ Date _____

Today I am **Grateful** for:

_____

_____

_____

_____

_____

_____

*"A little "thank you" that you will say to someone for
a "little favour" shown to you is a key to unlock the
doors that hide unseen "greater favours". Learn to
say "thank you" and why not?"*
— Israelmore Ayivor

Day _____ Date _____

Today I am **Grateful** for:

_____

_____

_____

_____

_____

_____

_____

Day _____ Date _____

Today I am **Grateful** for:

"Gratitude always comes into play; research shows that people are happier if they are grateful for the positive things in their lives, rather than worrying about what might be missing."
— Dan Buettner

Day _____ Date _____

Today I am **Grateful** for:

Day _____ Date _____
Today I am **Grateful** for:

----

*"Summoning gratitude is a sure way to get our life
back on track. Opening our eyes to affirm gratitude
grows the garden of our inner abundance, just as
standing close to a fire eventually warms our heart."*
— Alexandra Katehakis

Day _____ Date _____
Today I am **Grateful** for:

Day _____ Date _____

Today I am **Grateful** for:

_____

_____

_____

_____

_____

_____

"When you express gratitude for the blessings that
come into your life, it not only encourages the
universe to send you more, it also sees to it
that those blessings remain."
— Stephen Richards

Day _____ Date _____

Today I am **Grateful** for:

_____

_____

_____

_____

_____

_____

Day _____ Date _____

Today I am **Grateful** for:

"Gratitude and love are always multiplied when you
give freely. It is an infinite source of contentment
and prosperous energy."
— Jim Fargiano

Day _____ Date _____

Today I am **Grateful** for:

Day _____ Date _____

Today I am **Grateful** for:

_____

_____

_____

_____

_____

_____

"Don't count your blessings, let your blessings count!
Enjoy Life!"
— Bernard Kelvin Clive

Day _____ Date _____

Today I am **Grateful** for:

_____

_____

_____

_____

_____

_____

Day _____ Date _____

Today I am **Grateful** for:

_____

_____

_____

_____

_____

_____

"Most of us forget to take time for wonder, praise and gratitude until it is almost too late. Gratitude is a many-colored quality, reaching in all directions. It goes out for small things and for large; it is a God-ward going." — Faith Baldwin

Day _____ Date _____

Today I am **Grateful** for:

_____

_____

_____

_____

_____

_____

_____

Day _____ Date _____

Today I am **Grateful** for:

_____

_____

_____

_____

_____

_____

"No one can obtain felicity by pursuit. This explains
why one of the elements of being happy is the feeling
that a debt of gratitude is owed, a debt impossible to
pay. Now, we do not owe gratitude to ourselves. To be
conscious of gratitude is to acknowledge a gift."
— Josef Pieper

Day _____ Date _____

Today I am **Grateful** for:

_____

_____

_____

_____

_____

_____

_____

Day _____ Date _____

Today I am **Grateful** for:

_____

_____

_____

_____

_____

_____

"When I think of how many people in this world have
it worse than I do, I realize just how blessed I really
am...... and I have to give thanks ..."
— Shannan Lea

Day _____ Date _____

Today I am **Grateful** for:

_____

_____

_____

_____

_____

_____

_____

Day _____ Date _____

Today I am **Grateful** for:

----

*"I try hard to hold fast to the truth that a full and
thankful heart cannot entertain great conceits.
When brimming with gratitude, one's heartbeat
must surely result in outgoing love, the finest
emotion we can ever know."*
— Bill W

Day _____ Date _____

Today I am **Grateful** for:

Day _____ Date _____

Today I am **Grateful** for:

_____

_____

_____

_____

_____

_____

"Though they only take a second to say, thank yous
leave a warm feeling behind that can last for hours."
— Kent Allan Rees

Day _____ Date _____

Today I am **Grateful** for:

_____

_____

_____

_____

_____

_____

Day _____ Date _____

Today I am **Grateful** for:

_____

_____

_____

_____

_____

_____

"Lord I thank you for the gift of breath, eyes to see, ears to hear, tongue to taste, nose to smell, mouth to speak, face to smile, voice to sing, body to dance, legs to walk, mind to think and hands to write."
— Lailah Gifty Akita

Day _____ Date _____

Today I am **Grateful** for:

_____

_____

_____

_____

_____

_____

Day _____ Date _____

Today I am **Grateful** for:

_____

_____

_____

_____

_____

_____

"Gratitude is the antidote for misery. When you are counting your blessings you are too busy to be counting your problems."
— Miya Yamanouchi

Day _____ Date _____

Today I am **Grateful** for:

_____

_____

_____

_____

_____

_____

_____

Day _____ Date _____

Today I am **Grateful** for:

_____

_____

_____

_____

_____

_____

"The greatest of blessings can come from what appear
to be the smallest and most insignificant of things.
Don't discredit anything or anyone. One person, one
tiny thing, one little shift can change your life in
enormous ways." — Patience W. Smith

Day _____ Date _____

Today I am **Grateful** for:

_____

_____

_____

_____

_____

_____

Day _____ Date _____

Today I am **Grateful** for:

_____

_____

_____

_____

_____

_____

"Gratitude is a divine shift in your perspective from one of separation and lack to one of unity and right mindedness. It is a choice not made from guilt but rather from a higher level of consciousness."
— Janet Rebhan

Day _____ Date _____

Today I am **Grateful** for:

_____

_____

_____

_____

_____

_____

Day _____ Date _____

Today I am **Grateful** for:

_____

_____

_____

_____

_____

_____

"Gratitude is a divine emotion. It fills the heart, not to bursting; it warms it, but not to fever. I like to taste leisurely of bliss. Devoured in haste, I do not know its flavor."— Charlotte Brontë

Day _____ Date _____

Today I am **Grateful** for:

_____

_____

_____

_____

_____

_____

_____

Day _____ Date _____

Today I am **Grateful** for:

_____

_____

_____

_____

_____

_____

*"Road accidents, psycho-killings, plane crashes
abound - we don't know which day will be our last,
so why not make today the happiest day and be
thankful for all that we have?"*
— Maddy Malhotra

Day _____ Date _____

Today I am **Grateful** for:

_____

_____

_____

_____

_____

_____

Day _____ Date _____

Today I am **Grateful** for:

"Gratitude for all the beauty and blessings that we already enjoy fills our lives with abundance."
— Debasish Mridha

Day _____ Date _____

Today I am **Grateful** for:

Day _____ Date _____

Today I am **Grateful** for:

_____

_____

_____

_____

_____

_____

"Be grateful for what you already have while you
pursue what you want."
— Roy Bennett

Day _____ Date _____

Today I am **Grateful** for:

_____

_____

_____

_____

_____

_____

_____

Day _____ Date _____

Today I am **Grateful** for:

"By talking to yourself every hour of the day, you can
direct yourself to think thoughts of courage and
happiness, thoughts of power and peace. By talking
to yourself about the things you have to be grateful
for, you can fill your mind with thoughts that soar
and sing." — Dale Carnegie

Day _____ Date _____

Today I am **Grateful** for:

Day _____ Date _____

Today I am **Grateful** for:

_____

_____

_____

_____

_____

_____

*"Practice appreciation for who you are and what you
have... and allow your life to unfold in the most
amazing way."*
— Millen Livis

Day _____ Date _____

Today I am **Grateful** for:

_____

_____

_____

_____

_____

_____

_____

Day _____ Date _____

Today I am **Grateful** for:

_____

_____

_____

_____

_____

_____

*"When you overlook the small blessings in your life,
chances are that no amount of blessings would ever
make you happy."*
— Edmond Mbiaka

Day _____ Date _____

Today I am **Grateful** for:

_____

_____

_____

_____

_____

_____

Day _____ Date _____

Today I am **Grateful** for:

_____

_____

_____

_____

_____

_____

"Amidst all the bacchanal and confusion in your life, find something to be grateful for, even if it is the air that you breathe and trust me, this will transform you in some small way. Gratitude is really the great multiplier." — Akosua Dardaine Edwards

Day _____ Date _____

Today I am **Grateful** for:

_____

_____

_____

_____

_____

_____

_____

Day _____ Date _____

Today I am *Grateful* for:

----

*"Always remember people who have helped you along
the way, and don't forget to lift someone up."*
— Roy Bennett

Day _____ Date _____

Today I am *Grateful* for:

Day _____   Date _____

Today I am **Grateful** for:

_____

_____

_____

_____

_____

_____

"Gratitude, like faith, is a muscle. The more you use it, the stronger it grows, and the more power you have to use it on your behalf.. To be grateful is to find blessings in everything. This is the most powerful attitude to adopt, for there are blessings in everything." — Alan Cohen

Day _____   Date _____

Today I am **Grateful** for:

_____

_____

_____

_____

_____

_____

Day _____ Date _____

Today I am **Grateful** for:

"Gratitude opens our eyes to miracles that surround
us. Life's a miracle and a gift. Take every
breath in gratitude"
— D. Denise Dianaty

Day _____ Date _____

Today I am **Grateful** for:

Day _____ Date _____

Today I am **Grateful** for:

_____

_____

_____

_____

_____

_____

*"Throughout the day, anytime you find yourself
feeling stressed or wanting to complain, stop for 10
seconds and breathe. Count your breaths
and your blessings."*
— Jon Gordon

Day _____ Date _____

Today I am **Grateful** for:

_____

_____

_____

_____

_____

_____

_____

Day _____ Date _____

Today I am **Grateful** for:

_____

_____

_____

_____

_____

_____

"Approach the goal you've set with a positive, grateful
attitude, and your perception about the goal and
the journey will feel less like work, and more like
fun." — John Manning

Day _____ Date _____

Today I am **Grateful** for:

_____

_____

_____

_____

_____

_____

_____

Day _____ Date _____

Today I am **Grateful** for:

_____

_____

_____

_____

_____

_____

"Focus on your daily blessings, future opportunities and possibilities, and never allow your challenges, struggles, and obstacles to interfere with your peace of mind. You owe abundant happiness and success to your inner-self." — Edmond Mbiaka

Day _____ Date _____

Today I am **Grateful** for:

_____

_____

_____

_____

_____

_____

_____

Day _____ Date _____

Today I am **Grateful** for:

_____

_____

_____

_____

_____

_____

"This morning I woke up, how blessed I am
Eyes to see, a voice to speak
Words to read and love to feel?
If this isn't something to be thankful for, I'm not sure
what is." — Nikki Rowe

Day _____ Date _____

Today I am **Grateful** for:

_____

_____

_____

_____

_____

_____

_____

Day _____ Date _____

Today I am **Grateful** for:

----

*"... most of my prayers are expressions of sheer
gratitude for the fullness of my contentment."*
— Elizabeth Gilbert

Day _____ Date _____

Today I am **Grateful** for:

Day _____ Date _____

Today I am **Grateful** for:

"When you arise in the morning, give thanks for the morning light, for your life and strength. Give thanks for your food and the joy of living, If you see no reason for giving thanks, the fault lies with yourself." — Tecumseh

Day _____ Date _____

Today I am **Grateful** for:

Day _____ Date _____

Today I am **Grateful** for:

_____

_____

_____

_____

_____

_____

*"Gratitude is the key to manifestation, for gratitude
connects you directly to the source.
Keep your head up and heart open. And make
"Thank You" your mantra of life!
— Abhishek Kumar*

Day _____ Date _____

Today I am **Grateful** for:

_____

_____

_____

_____

_____

_____

Day _____ Date _____

Today I am **Grateful** for:

_____

_____

_____

_____

_____

_____

"When last did u sit back and took an opportunity to lookup and thank the Heavens above for blessing you with what you have and continuing to open doors for you every time you knock "and sometimes letting you in through the window" because not all doors are as beautiful on the inside as they are on the inside" — Katlego Semusa

Day _____ Date _____

Today I am **Grateful** for:

_____

_____

_____

_____

_____

_____

_____

Day _____ Date _____

Today I am **Grateful** for:

"The most fortunate are those who have a wonderful capacity to appreciate again and again, freshly and naively, the basic goods of life, with awe, pleasure, wonder and even ecstasy."
— Abraham Maslow

Day _____ Date _____

Today I am **Grateful** for:

Day _____ Date _____

Today I am **Grateful** for:

----

*"Feeling entitled is the opposite of feeling grateful.
Gratitude opens the heart, entitlement closes it."*
— Paul Gibbons

Day _____ Date _____

Today I am **Grateful** for:

Day _____ Date _____

Today I am **Grateful** for:

_____

_____

_____

_____

_____

_____

*"Gratitude should run through our veins, it
should reside in us, it should live in
our bones as long we live."*
— Euginia Herlihy

Day _____ Date _____

Today I am **Grateful** for:

_____

_____

_____

_____

_____

_____

_____

Day _____   Date _____

Today I am **Grateful** for:

"The more we express thanks, the more gratitude we feel. The more gratitude we feel, the more we express thanks. It's circular, and it leads to a happier life."
— *Steve Goodier*

Day _____   Date _____

Today I am **Grateful** for:

Day _____ Date _____

Today I am **Grateful** for:

_____

_____

_____

_____

_____

_____

"If I do not feel a sense of joy in God's creation, if I
forget to offer the world back to God with
thankfulness, I have advanced very little upon the
Way. I have not yet learnt to be truly human. For it is
only through thanksgiving that I can become
myself." — Kallistos Ware

Day _____ Date _____

Today I am **Grateful** for:

_____

_____

_____

_____

_____

_____

_____

Day _____ Date _____

Today I am **Grateful** for:

_____

_____

_____

_____

_____

_____

"There is no prescription for finding moments of gratitude in every day; there is simply the choice."
— Gillian Deacon

Day _____ Date _____

Today I am **Grateful** for:

_____

_____

_____

_____

_____

_____

Day _____ Date _____

Today I am **Grateful** for:

"We all feel better when we are grateful. There is
great wisdom in understanding that no matter the
situation, there is always something for which we
can choose to be grateful."
— Andy Andrews

Day _____ Date _____

Today I am **Grateful** for:

Day _____ Date _____

Today I am **Grateful** for:

"The most beautiful moments in life are moments when you are expressing your joy, not when you are seeking it."
— Jaggi Vasudev

Day _____ Date _____

Today I am **Grateful** for:

Day _____ Date _____

Today I am **Grateful** for:

_____

_____

_____

_____

_____

_____

*"Grow in a way without losing much of our inner
childlike deep senses embracing truthful, pure,
simple relief of appreciation and gratitude."*
— Angelica Hopes

Day _____ Date _____

Today I am **Grateful** for:

_____

_____

_____

_____

_____

_____

Day _____ Date _____

Today I am **Grateful** for:

"Feeling grateful is good; showing appreciation to those you feel grateful to is sublime."
— Andy Lacroix

Day _____ Date _____

Today I am **Grateful** for:

Day _____ Date _____

Today I am **Grateful** for:

_____

_____

_____

_____

_____

_____

"Be grateful for life. Show gratitude to others,
whether it's verbally or energetically, it has
the same effect."
— Kasi Kaye Iliopoulos

Day _____ Date _____

Today I am **Grateful** for:

_____

_____

_____

_____

_____

_____

_____

Day _____ Date _____

Today I am **Grateful** for:

_____

_____

_____

_____

_____

_____

"I count myself lucky, having long ago won a lottery
paid to me in seven sunrises a week for life."
— Robert Brault

Day _____ Date _____

Today I am **Grateful** for:

_____

_____

_____

_____

_____

_____

Day _____ Date _____

Today I am **Grateful** for:

_____

_____

_____

_____

_____

_____

1. Woke up ✓
2. Air to breath ✓
3. Food to eat ✓
4. Roof over head ✓
...yep, it's a Good day!"
— Russell Kyle

Day _____ Date _____

Today I am **Grateful** for:

_____

_____

_____

_____

_____

_____

Day _____ Date _____

Today I am **Grateful** for:

----

*"The Power of Thank You goes a very long way! Its
healing embodiment of gratitude is a key element to
living a happier life."*
— Angie Karan Krezos

Day _____ Date _____

Today I am **Grateful** for:

Day _____ Date _____

Today I am **Grateful** for:

_____

_____

_____

_____

_____

_____

"Nothing is so fundamental to the spiritual life as
learning to give thanks."
— Gordon T. Smith

Day _____ Date _____

Today I am **Grateful** for:

_____

_____

_____

_____

_____

_____

Day _____ Date _____

Today I am **Grateful** for:

"When you open to your heart, your entire world changes--it opens up around you. You see yourself as part of a friendly universe, one that is full of possibility, one that is generating and regenerating a positive energy." — Baptist de Pape

Day _____ Date _____

Today I am **Grateful** for:

Day _____ Date _____

Today I am **Grateful** for:

_____

_____

_____

_____

_____

_____

*"You must love yourself first to the soul
of your aura..."*
— Jennifer Pierre

Day _____ Date _____

Today I am **Grateful** for:

_____

_____

_____

_____

_____

_____

Day _____ Date _____

Today I am **Grateful** for:

_____

_____

_____

_____

_____

_____

"The height of our success is marked at the depth of
our gratitude."
— Terry Crouson

Day _____ Date _____

Today I am **Grateful** for:

_____

_____

_____

_____

_____

_____

Day _____ Date _____

Today I am **Grateful** for:

_____

_____

_____

_____

_____

_____

*"If the heights of our joy are measured by the depths
of our gratitude, and gratitude is but a way of
seeing, a spiritual perspective of smallness might offer
a vital way of seeing especially conducive to
gratitude"* — Ann Voskamp

Day _____ Date _____

Today I am **Grateful** for:

_____

_____

_____

_____

_____

_____

Day _____ Date _____

Today I am **Grateful** for:

"When your heart aligns with the truth of its energy, GRATITUDE sings your name, LOVE flows freely, and every bit of your being is awakened, breathing and moving in perfect HARMONY."
— Angie Karan Krezos

Day _____ Date _____

Today I am **Grateful** for:

Day _____ Date _____

Today I am **Grateful** for:

_____

_____

_____

_____

_____

_____

"Just as thoughts, send out vibrations to which there is a creative and attractive power, gratitude stimulates the field of etheric energy that surrounds you on a subtle level to bring into your life more of what brings you joy."— Genevieve Gerard

Day _____ Date _____

Today I am **Grateful** for:

_____

_____

_____

_____

_____

_____

Day _____ Date _____

Today I am **Grateful** for:

_____

_____

_____

_____

_____

_____

"Never let them try out this gratitude, for they would immediately discover that it supplies the first and most important component to happiness: Contentment."
— Geoffrey Wood

Day _____ Date _____

Today I am **Grateful** for:

_____

_____

_____

_____

_____

Day _____ Date _____

Today I am **Grateful** for:

_____

_____

_____

_____

_____

_____

"The good news is that being in gratitude does not require time and money. All it requires is an attitude of being grateful."
— Vishwas Chavan

Day _____ Date _____

Today I am **Grateful** for:

_____

_____

_____

_____

_____

_____

Day _____ Date _____

Today I am **Grateful** for:

"Love is such a deep gratitude. When you are truly in
love with life, every breath you take is gratitude."
— *Bryant McGill*

Day _____ Date _____

Today I am **Grateful** for:

Day _____ Date _____

Today I am **Grateful** for:

_____

_____

_____

_____

_____

_____

*"Being able to appreciate who we are and what we
have in the now is an easy way to journey
through this life."*
— Raphael Zernoff

Day _____ Date _____

Today I am **Grateful** for:

_____

_____

_____

_____

_____

_____

Day _____ Date _____

Today I am **Grateful** for:

"As we express our gratitude, we must never forget
that the highest appreciation is not to utter words,
but to live by them."
— John F. Kennedy

Day _____ Date _____

Today I am **Grateful** for:

Day _____ Date _____

Today I am **Grateful** for:

_____

_____

_____

_____

_____

_____

"Gratitude is the heart of humility, and humility is
the path to peace, love, and understanding."
— Justin Young

Day _____ Date _____

Today I am **Grateful** for:

_____

_____

_____

_____

_____

_____

Day _____ Date _____

Today I am **Grateful** for:

"How would your life be different if you celebrated the things in your life that you do have instead of lamenting things that you don't? Let today be the day you embrace gratitude and appreciation and let go of entitlement and expectation."
— Steve Maraboli

Day _____ Date _____

Today I am **Grateful** for:

Day _____ Date _____

Today I am **Grateful** for:

_____

_____

_____

_____

_____

_____

"With all respect to your religion or world-view —
thank God, thank the universe, thank evolutionary
processes — the keyword is "thank" — just have some
gratitude and be thankful."
— Bryant McGill

Day _____ Date _____

Today I am **Grateful** for:

_____

_____

_____

_____

_____

_____

Day _____ Date _____

Today I am **Grateful** for:

_____

_____

_____

_____

_____

_____

"Embrace the change you desperately need. Tear
down your walls and show gratitude for little
things." — J Loren Norris

Day _____ Date _____

Today I am **Grateful** for:

_____

_____

_____

_____

_____

_____

Day _____ Date _____

Today I am **Grateful** for:

_____

_____

_____

_____

_____

_____

"Gratitude is an excellent attitude which can lift you
to a greater altitude if you put it on as a vesture."
— S. E. Entsua-Mensah

Day _____ Date _____

Today I am **Grateful** for:

_____

_____

_____

_____

_____

_____

Day _____ Date _____

Today I am **Grateful** for:

_____

_____

_____

_____

_____

_____

"The moment that you give gratitude is the moment
that you find happiness. The moment that you lose
gratitude your happiness will vanish and slip
through your fingers" — Rasheed Ogunlaru

Day _____ Date _____

Today I am **Grateful** for:

_____

_____

_____

_____

_____

_____

Day _____ Date _____

Today I am **Grateful** for:

"Gratitude is not just a word; it is a way of life."
— Rob Martin

Day _____ Date _____

Today I am **Grateful** for:

Day _____ Date _____

Today I am **Grateful** for:

_____

_____

_____

_____

_____

_____

"I live by three simple words: compassion, love and gratitude. We need to act on these three words daily. Doing so will irrevocably change your world."
— Julian Pencilliah

Day _____ Date _____

Today I am **Grateful** for:

_____

_____

_____

_____

_____

_____

Day _____ Date _____

Today I am **Grateful** for:

_____

_____

_____

_____

_____

_____

*"This is a wonderful day. I've never seen
this one before."*
— Maya Angelou

Day _____ Date _____

Today I am **Grateful** for:

_____

_____

_____

_____

_____

_____

Day _____ Date _____

Today I am **Grateful** for:

_____

_____

_____

_____

_____

_____

"Find magic in the little things, and the big things
you always expected will start to show up."
— Isa Zapata

Day _____ Date _____

Today I am **Grateful** for:

_____

_____

_____

_____

_____

_____

Day _____ Date _____

Today I am **Grateful** for:

_____

_____

_____

_____

_____

_____

"If we all counted our blessings and then shared
them with our neighbors, near and far,
all our lives would be richer."
— Janet Autherine

Day _____ Date _____

Today I am **Grateful** for:

_____

_____

_____

_____

_____

_____

Day _____ Date _____

Today I am **Grateful** for:

_____

_____

_____

_____

_____

_____

"Amazement + Gratitude + Openness + Appreciation =
an irresistible field of energy"
— Frederick Dodson

Day _____ Date _____

Today I am **Grateful** for:

_____

_____

_____

_____

_____

_____

Day _____ Date _____

Today I am **Grateful** for:

_____

_____

_____

_____

_____

_____

*"You simply will not be the same person two months
from now after consciously giving thanks each day
for the abundance that exists in your life."*
— Sarah Ban Breathnach

Day _____ Date _____

Today I am **Grateful** for:

_____

_____

_____

_____

_____

_____

Day _____ Date _____

Today I am **Grateful** for:

"Everyday gratitude sweetens what appears flavorless
and brightens all that appears dim."
— Amy Leigh Mercree

Day _____ Date _____

Today I am **Grateful** for:

Day _____ Date _____

Today I am **Grateful** for:

_____

_____

_____

_____

_____

_____

"Every day, tell at least one person something you
like, admire, or appreciate about them."
— Richard Carlson

Day _____ Date _____

Today I am **Grateful** for:

_____

_____

_____

_____

_____

_____

Day _____ Date _____

Today I am **Grateful** for:

_____

_____

_____

_____

_____

_____

*"In life, as in knitting, don't leave loose ends. Take
the time to thank the people who matter in your life."*
— Reba Linker

Day _____ Date _____

Today I am **Grateful** for:

_____

_____

_____

_____

_____

_____

Day _____ Date _____

Today I am **Grateful** for:

_____

_____

_____

_____

_____

_____

"Gratitude makes you a better, stronger, wiser person.
Ingratitude makes you a negative, angry, miserable
person. Which person do you choose to be?"
— Tanya Masse

Day _____ Date _____

Today I am **Grateful** for:

_____

_____

_____

_____

_____

_____

Day _____ Date _____

Today I am **Grateful** for:

_____

_____

_____

_____

_____

_____

"What I've learned is there's a scientifically proven
phenomenon that's attached to gratitude, and that
if you consciously take note of what is good in your
life, quantifiable benefits happen."
— Deborah Norville

Day _____ Date _____

Today I am **Grateful** for:

_____

_____

_____

_____

_____

_____

Day _____ Date _____

Today I am **Grateful** for:

_____

_____

_____

_____

_____

_____

"Gratitude is not something idyllic that comes when all good things line up to be counted. Gratitude is there all the time waiting to be focused on."
— Antonia Montoya

Day _____ Date _____

Today I am **Grateful** for:

_____

_____

_____

_____

_____

_____

Day _____ Date _____

Today I am **Grateful** for:

_____

_____

_____

_____

_____

_____

"If we do not feel grateful for what we already have,
what makes us think we would be happy with more?"
— John A. Passaro

Day _____ Date _____

Today I am **Grateful** for:

_____

_____

_____

_____

_____

_____

Day _____ Date _____

Today I am **Grateful** for:

_____

_____

_____

_____

_____

_____

"Thankfulness is the beginning of gratitude.
Gratitude is the completion of thankfulness.
Thankfulness may consist merely of words.
Gratitude is shown in acts."
— Henri-Frédéric Amiel

Day _____ Date _____

Today I am **Grateful** for:

_____

_____

_____

_____

_____

_____

Need another 5 Minute Gratitude Journal?
Visit www.blankbooksnjournals.com

27704601R00062

Made in the USA
San Bernardino, CA
17 December 2015